How to ace your German oral

Questions and answers on all topics
With English translation and glossary

Lucy's dedication:

My father taught me the basics of German over the Christmas holidays when I was changing schools at thirteen. This book is dedicated to him. I will never forget a story he told about meeting an ex-army officer on the train to school, a few years after the war. The officer saw the German book in his hand and smiled

"Easy German – Bahnhof, Krankenhaus".

If only that was all you had to know....

Susanna's dedication:

Time and again German has come into my life, from birth to six years and the heady influence of my friend's Swiss German mother - on whom I modelled an alter ego to escape into a fantasy world, full of pretend Swiss German - to long walks in the Black Forest with family friends, where it was all Grüss Gott and ripping Lebkuchen off the Knusperhaus. It's perhaps no coincidence that some of my closest friends, Chris, Audrie and Rokaya, have a strong German connection, and it is to their enduring friendship that I dedicate this book, without forgetting that, as with most good things that happened to me, it all started with my parents.

Table of contents

Introduction

In this book we have combined all the standard oral questions and produced a set of answers together with an English translation and glossary of key phrases. One size does not fit all, and you may wish to cut and paste, pick and choose which answers or phrases you include in your own work. You may need to change the description of your family, town and school in order to be factually correct but the overall structures and expressions can still be included.

It's not cheating!

Languages are hard to learn in a classroom, and teachers rarely have enough time to give each student the one-to-one time they need for oral practice. There are plenty of students out there getting help outside school, and here's your chance to be one of them.

Children learn by hearing and copying, and that's what is happening here. Once those phrases are stuck in your head, you'll be able to use them not only in the oral exam but out and about in real life. To make the most of the learning experience, test yourself by looking at the English and translating it into German, then checking with the German text.

There is a positive thread running throughout the answers. If you use them word for word you will end up sounding like a super-hardworking clean-living tennis fiend with a strong environmental awareness and an abundance of energy. Even if this isn't you, pretending that it is will give you a chance to use some great idioms.

Using this book, you can replace a boring sentence like "I live in London" earning you no points at all, to something much more eye-catching like "I'm lucky because I've been living in London for 5 years and it's the best city in the world."

All these examiner-pleasing structures are listed in the glossary, so test yourself on the glossary pages to get an intensive immersion experience in the top phrases. As I tell my students, you should fire these impressive expressions at the examiner like a machine gun, not just in the oral, but in your writing as well, and you'll be well on the way to top marks.

So what are you waiting for? Go knock 'em dead!

Lucy and Susanna

INTRODUCING YOURSELF

About you

Ich heiße ………. und ich bin … .. Jahre alt. Ich bin ziemlich groß, ich habe blonde Haare und blaue Augen. Ich bin sehr lustig, sportlich und intelligent, aber manchmal bin ich ein bisschen faul, besonders morgens, wenn ich nicht in die Schule will.

My name is ………. and I'm ….. years old. I am quite tall, I have blonde hair and blue eyes. I am very funny, sporty, and intelligent but sometimes a bit lazy, especially in the mornings when I don't want to go to school.

About your interests and hobbies

Wenn ich Zeit habe, mag ich mit meinem Vater Radfahren. Am Wochenende spiele ich mit meinem Freund im Park Tennis, weil es mein Lieblingssport ist, und ich total versessen bin. Ich habe Glück, weil ich seit zwei Jahren Mitglied eines Tennisclubs bin. Um mich zu entspannen und um den Stress der Schule zu vergessen, sehe ich viel Fern, obwohl es gesundheitsschädlich ist. Ich möchte gerne Schach lernen, weil es interessanter scheint, als den ganzen Tag vor dem Fernseher zu verbringen.

When I have time, I like to go cycling with my father and at the weekends I play tennis with my friend in the park because it's my favourite sport and I'm addicted to it. I'm lucky because I have been a member of a tennis club for 2 years. I spend a lot of time watching TV, although it is bad for your health, in order to relax and to forget the stress of school. I'd like to learn chess because it seems more interesting than spending all day watching TV.

Your family

Wir sind fünf Familienmitglieder: meine Mutter, mein Vater, meine zwei Brüder und ich. Mein älterer Bruder ist groß, schlank, gutaussehend und spörtlicher als ich. Er hat braune Haare und grüne Augen. Er spielt gern Fußball und schwimmt gern. Mein jüngerer Bruder hat blonde Haare und blaue Augen. Wir sehen uns sehr ähnlich aus und wir verstehen uns gut, weil wir die gleiche Musik mögen, aber er kann auch sehr nervig sein. Ich komme mit meinen Eltern ganz gut aus, aber manchmal streiten wir, weil sie es nicht mögen, wenn ich spät nach Hause komme.

In my family there are 5 people: my mother, my father, my two brothers and me. My older brother is tall, slim, very handsome and sportier than me. He has brown hair and green eyes. He likes playing football and going swimming. My younger brother has blond hair and blue eyes. We look very similar and we get on well, because we like the same music but he can also be very annoying. I get on quite well with my parents, but sometimes we argue because they don't like it when I come home late.

HOUSE, HOME AND DAILY ROUTINE

Your house

Meiner Meinung nach, ist mein Haus das beste Haus der Welt, und ich wohne darin schon seit fünf Jahren. Mein Haus ist groß, modern und komfortabel. Im Erdgeschoß gibt es die Küche, das Wohnzimmer, das Büro und das Esszimmer. Auf der ersten Etage befinden sich vier Schlafzimmer und ein Badezimmer. Hinter dem Haus ist ein großer Garten, in dem man Fußball spielen kann, wenn es gutes Wetter ist. Am besten gefällt mir, dass ich mein Schlafzimmer mit meinem Bruder nicht mehr teilen muss, weil er so nervig ist.

In my opinion my house is the best house in the world and I have been living there for 5 years. My house is big, modern and comfortable. On the ground floor there is the kitchen, the lounge, the office and the dining room. On the first floor there are four bedrooms and a bathroom. Behind the house is a big garden where you can play football when it is good weather. What I like most is that I no longer have to share my bedroom with my brother because he is so annoying.

Your bedroom

Mein Schlafzimmer befindet sich im ersten Stock, neben dem Schlafzimmer meiner Eltern. Neben dem Bett steht ein Schrank und vor dem Fenster steht ein Schreibtisch, an dem ich meine Hausaufgaben mache. Die Wände sind in meiner Lieblingsfarbe blau gestrichen und ich habe glücklicherweise nicht nur einen

Laptop, sondern auch einen Fernseher, und kann deshalb locker stundenlang dahoch bleiben, ohne nach unten gehen zu müßen.

My bedroom is on the first floor by my parents' bedroom. Next to the bed there is a cupboard and in front of the window is a desk where I do my homework. The walls are blue because it's my favourite colour and I'm lucky because I not only have a laptop but also a television so I can easily spend many hours relaxing without having to go downstairs.

Where you lived when you were young

Als ich jung war, wohnte ich in einem kleinen Haus auf dem Land. Es gab einen großen Garten hinter dem Haus, wo ich jeden Tag Fußball spielte, weil ich so sportlich war. Ich hatte einen Hund und musste jeden Tag mit dem Hund raus.

When I was young I lived in a small house in the countryside. There was a big garden behind the house where I played football every day because I was so sporty. I had a dog and had to walk it every day.

Ideal house

Wenn ich reich wäre, würde ich mein Traumhaus kaufen. Mein Traumhaus wäre sehr groß, modern und komfortabel, mit einem großen Schwimmbad, damit ich jeden Tag schwimmen könnte. Wenn ich wirklich reich wäre, hätte ich auch ein Kino, in dem ich viele Stunden mit meinen Freunden verbringen würde. Es wäre in der Nähe des Zentrums von London, damit meine Freunde mich besuchen könnten.

If I were rich I would buy my ideal house. My ideal house would be enormous, modern and comfortable with a big pool so I could swim every day. If I was really rich there would also be a cinema where I would spend many hours with my friends. It would be near the centre of London so that my friends could visit me.

What is the ideal family?

Ich glaube nicht, dass es die ideale Familie gibt - sondern, dass ein Kind Liebe und Stabilität braucht und der Familientyp keine Rolle spielt. Das wichtigste ist, dass man sich auf seine Familie verlassen kann. Heutzutage gibt es viele verschiedene Arten von Familien - homosexuelle Paare, Alleinerziehende, traditionelle Familien, große Familien und alle haben ihren Wert.

I don't think there is such a thing as the ideal family – just that a child needs love and stability and the type of family doesn't matter. The important thing is to be able to rely on your family. Nowadays there are loads of different types of family – with homosexual couples, single parents, traditional families, large families, and all have their value.

Is marriage important?

Es hängt davon ab, ob Sie religiös sind. Meiner Meinung nach, spielt es keine Rolle, ob man verheiratet ist oder nicht, vor allem, da viele Ehen scheitern und die Anzahl Singles steigt. Ich weiß nicht, ob ich heiraten werde oder nicht. Ich möchte für ein paar Jahre mit jemandem zusammenleben, bevor ich eine solch wichtige Entscheidung treffe. Wir sollten mehr über Beziehungen in der Schule lernen, damit wir wissen, was die Ehe mit sich bringt.

It depends on whether you are religious or not. In my opinion, it doesn't matter if you are married or not, especially because so many marriages break down and the number of single people is increasing. I don't know if I will get married or not. I'd like to live with someone for a few years before making such an important decision. We should learn more about relationships at school so that we know what marriage involves.

Describe your best friend

Ich habe Glück, weil ich <u>den</u> besten Freund der Welt habe. Er heißt .... und er ist .... Jahre alt. Wir sind schon seit zehn Jahren Freunde. Er hat blaue Augen und blonde Haare. Er ist größer als ich, aber nicht ganz so sportlich. Wir verstehen uns gut, weil wir viele gemeinsame Hobbys haben - wir mögen Videospiele, und wir gehen am Wochenende zusammen einkaufen. Wir haben auch den gleichen Humor. Wir sind total auf einer Wellenlänge! Das Einzige ist, dass er nicht gerne Fußball spielt und ich ein Man United Fan bin. Wenn er nur Fußball spielen würde, wäre er perfekt.

I am lucky because I have the best friend in the world He is called .... and he is .... years old. We have been friends for ten years. He has blue eyes and blonde hair. He is taller than me, but less sporty. We get on well because we have lots of hobbies in common – we like videogames and we usually go shopping together at the weekend. Also we have the same sense of humour. How lucky! The only thing is that he doesn't like football and I'm a Man United fan. If he played football he would be perfect.

Recent outing with best friend

Letztes Wochenende bin ich mit .... in London einkaufen gegangen. Ich musste ein Geburtstagsgeschenk für meine Mutter kaufen. Als wir in die Stadtmitte angekommen sind, haben wir eine Menge Kleidung gekauft und sind danach zum Mittagessen in eine Pizzeria gegangen. Das Schlimme war, dass ich fast vergessen habe, das Geschenk für meine Mutter zu kaufen. Zum Glück, gibt es ein Geschäft in der Nähe meines Hauses, in dem man interessante Naturbücher kaufen kann. Ich habe ein Buch gekauft und bin nach Hause zurückgekehrt. Es hat meiner Mutter sehr gut gefallen.

Last weekend I went with .... to London to go shopping. I had to buy a present for my mother for her birthday. On arriving in the centre, we bought a lot of clothes and afterwards we ate lunch in a pizzeria. The bad thing was that I almost forgot to buy a present for my mother. Luckily there is a shop near my house where they sell interesting books on nature. I chose a book, bought it and went home. My mother really loved it.

Future outing with best friend

Nächstes Wochenende werden wir neue Kleidung kaufen gehen. Danach werden wir den neuen James Bond Film im Kino ansehen, weil wir Action-Filme lieben. Bevor wir nach Haus zurückgehen, werden wir unsere Schulfreunde zum Abendessen in einem Restaurant treffen und über den Film diskutieren.

Next weekend we are going to go shopping to look for new clothes. Afterwards we will go to the cinema to see the new Bond film because we love action films. Before going home, we will have dinner in a restaurant with our school friends and we will discuss the film.

Daily routine

Normalerweise muss ich am Morgen sehr früh aufstehen, weil ich in die Schule gehen muss. Ich wache um 7 Uhr auf und stehe auf. Zuerst dusche ich und ziehe mich vor dem Frühstück an. Ich nehme um 8 Uhr den Schulbus und wenn ich ankomme, rede ich mit meinen Freunden. Der Unterricht beginnt um neun Uhr und wir haben acht Unterrichtsstunden von 40 Minuten pro Tag. Ich gehe um 4.30 nach Hause, mache meine Hausaufgaben, esse mit meiner Familie und danach sehe ich entweder im Wohnzimmer fern oder chatte ich online mit meinen Freunden. Gegen 10 Uhr gehe ich ins Bett.

Normally in the morning I have to get up really early because I have to go to school. I wake up at 7, I get up, shower and get dressed before having breakfast. I go to school by bus at 8 and when I arrive I chat to my friends. Lessons begin at 9 and we have 8 lessons of 40 minutes each per day. I go home at 4.30, do my homework, eat with my family and after eating I usually watch TV in the lounge or chat online with my friends. I go to bed around 10.

Daily routine weekend

Am Wochenende stehe ich später auf, weil ich nicht in die Schule muss. Ich frühstücke um 11 Uhr und ich gehe mit meinen Freunden in den Park oder in die Shopping-Mall zum Einkaufen. Am Nachmittag spiele ich Tennis im Sportzentrum, und am Abend essen wir immer zusammen zu Hause. Manchmal sehen wir einen Film auf Netflix oder verbringen wir den Abend beim Kartenspielen. Ich brauche ein paar Stunden, meine Hausaufgaben fertig zu machen, aber in der Regel schiebe ich das bis zur letzten Minute auf.

At the weekend I get up later than usual because I don't have to go to school. I have breakfast around 11 and I go out with my friends to the park or the shopping mall to go shopping. In the afternoon I usually play tennis at the sports centre, and we always have dinner together as a family. Sometimes we watch a film on Netflix or we spend the evening playing cards. I spend a few hours doing my homework but I usually leave it until the last minute.

This morning

Heute morgen bin ich sehr früh aufgestanden, weil ich in die
Schule gehen musste. Ich habe geduscht, habe mich angezogen
und habe schnell gefrühstückt. Morgens muss ich immer ganz
schön hetzen um fertig zu sein. Ich bin mit dem Bus zur Schule
gefahren und bin um 8 Uhr angekommen. Ich habe mit meinen
Freunden geredet und habe ein bisschen mehr Revision für meine
Deutschprüfung gemacht.

*Today I got up really early because I had to go to school, I
showered, got dressed and had breakfast quickly before leaving. I
am always in a hurry in the morning. I went to school by bus and
arrived at 8. I chatted with my friends and did a bit more revision
for my Spanish oral exam.*

This evening

Wenn ich nach Hause komme, werde ich mich entspannen, bevor
ich meine Hausaufgaben mache. Ich werde fernsehen, und ich
werde versuchen, den Stress des Schultages zu vergessen. Wenn
ich nur könnte! Ich werde gegen 7 Uhr essen. Danach werde ich
mit meinen Schulfreunden in den sozialen Netzwerken chatten,
weil ich davon ganz **abhängig** bin, und ich es ohne Facebook und
Snapchat nicht aushalten kann.

*When I get home I'm going to relax before doing my homework. I
will watch TV and I will try to forget the stress of the school day. If
only I could! I will have dinner around 7. Afterwards I will chat*

with my school friends on social networks because I am addicted
and I can't manage without Facebook and Snapchat.

What you would change about your routine

Wenn es möglich wäre, würde ich die Hausaufgaben nicht
während der Woche machen. Jeden Abend habe ich zwei Stunden
Hausaufgaben zu tun, und ich bin immer müde und gestresst. Ich
möchte auch länger im Bett bleiben. Wissenschaftler sagen, dass
junge Menschen mehr Schlaf brauchen, und ich bin damit völlig
einverstanden. Die Schule sollte erst am Mittag beginnen.

If it were possible, I wouldn't do homework during the
week. Every evening I have to do two hours of homework and I
am always tired and stressed. Also I would like to stay in bed until
later. Scientists say that young people need more sleep and I am
completely in agreement. School should start at midday.

Helping at home

Um meinen Eltern zu helfen, wasche ich ab / wasche ich das Auto,
räume ich mein Zimmer auf, / decke den Tisch ab. Manchmal
koche ich. Aber es ist schwer die Zeit zu finden, weil die Lehrer
uns so viel Hausaufgaben geben, und ich verbringe viel Zeit beim
Lernen. Wenn ich weniger Hausaufgaben hätte, würde ich mehr
tun, um zu helfen.

To help my parents I wash the dishes / the car, I tidy my room, I
hoover, I lay / clear the table, I cook meals and sometimes I clean

the kitchen. However, I struggle to do it now because the teachers
give us so much homework and I spend a lot of time revising for
exams. If I had less homework I would do more to help.

Help at home yesterday

Gestern habe ich den Abwasch gemacht und mein Zimmer
aufgeräumt. Ich hätte mehr getan, wenn ich Zeit gehabt hätte,
aber die Lehrer geben uns zu viele Hausaufgaben.

Yesterday I washed the dishes, laid the table and tidied my
room. I would have done more if I had had time, but the teachers
give us too much homework.

Cooking at home

Normalerweise kocht meine Mutter, aber wenn sie nicht da ist,
tue ich es. Ich koche gerne, und wenn ich die Zeit hätte, würde ich
mehr tun, aber die Lehrer geben uns zu viele Hausaufgaben.

In general, my mother cooks the meals, but when she's not there, I
do it. I like cooking, and if I had the time I would do more, but the
teachers give us too much homework.

Plans for next weekend with family

Nächstes Wochenende möchte ich mit meinem Vater Radfahren,
weil wir beide Zeit an der frischen Luft genießen. Am Nachmittag
werde ich mit meiner Mutter einkaufen gehen. Danach werden

wir ins Kino gehen, um den neuen Bond-Film zu sehen, weil wir Action-Filme lieben. Bevor wir nach Hause gehen, werden wir den Film beim Abendessen in einem Restaurant diskutieren. Wenn ich nach Hause komme, werde ich ins Bett und ich werde wie ein Murmeltier schlafen.

Next weekend I'd like to go cycling with my dad because we like spending time in the fresh air. In the afternoon I'm going to go shopping with my mother. Afterwards we will go to the cinema to see the new Bond film because we love action films. Before going home, we will have dinner in a restaurant and discuss the film. When I get home I will go to bed and sleep like a log.

Recent family activity

Letztes Wochenende sind wir zum Fußballspielen in den Park gegangen, dann sind wir einkaufen gegangen, und danach sind wir nach Hause gegangen um zu essen. Wir haben den Nachmittag bei meinen Großeltern verbracht. Wir haben Tee getrunken und haben leckere Kuchen gegessen. Als wir zurückgekommen sind, haben wir beschlossen, einen Actionfilm zu sehen. Ich bin um 11 ins Bett gegangen und habe wie ein Murmeltier geschlafen.

Last weekend we went to the park to play football, walk the dog, we went shopping and then we went home to eat. In the afternoon we went to visit my grandparents who live near us, we had tea and ate delicious cakes. When we got back (on returning) we decided to watch an action film. I went to bed at 11 and slept like a log.

WHERE YOU LIVE

Describe your town

Ich habe Glück, weil ich seit zehn Jahren in London wohne und das ist die beste Stadt der Welt. Was ich am meisten mag ist, dass es viel zu unternehmen gibt. Man kann ins Kino oder ins Theater gehen, es gibt Restaurants, Museen und Geschäfte, Sportzentren und Parks, in denen man Tennis oder Fußball spielen kann. Normalerweise gehe ich jedes Wochenende ins Kino, weil ich auf Filme ganz verrückt bin.

I'm lucky because I've been living in London for ten years and it's the best city in the world. What I like most is that there is a lot to do. You can go to the cinema, to the theatre, to restaurants, to museums, and there are shops, sports centres, parks where you can play tennis or football. I usually go to the cinema every weekend because I love films.

Recent outing in town

Letztes Wochenende bin ich mit .... nach London einkaufen gegangen. Ich musste ein Geschenk für meine Mutter zu ihrem Geburtstag kaufen. Als wir in der Stadtmitte angekommen sind, haben wir eine Menge Kleidung gekauft und sind danach zum Mittagessen in einer Pizzeria gegangen. Das Schlimme war, dass ich fast vergessen habe, das Geschenk für meine Mutter zu kaufen. Zum Glück gibt es ein Geschäft in der Nähe meines Hauses, in dem man interessante Naturbücher kaufen kann. Ich habe ein Buch gekauft und bin nach Hause zurückgekehrt. Es hat meiner Mutter sehr gefallen.

Last weekend I went with .... to London to go shopping. I had to buy a presents for my mother for her birthday. On arriving in the centre, we bought a lot of clothes and afterwards we ate lunch in a pizzeria. The bad thing was that I almost forgot to buy a present for my mother. Luckily there is a shop near my house where they sell interesting books on nature. I chose a book, bought it and went home. My mother really loved it.

What is there for young people in your town?

Ich habe Glück, weil es eine Menge für junge Leute in meiner Umgebung zu tun gibt. Es gibt ein Sportzentrum, in dem man Sport treiben kann, ein Kino und viele Restaurants. Normalerweise gehe ich ins Kino oder spiele ich Tennis im Park. Das Schlimme ist, dass alles hier unheimlich teuer ist, und ich es mir nicht leisten kann. Es wäre perfekt, wenn es einen Ort gäbe, an dem sich junge Menschen treffen könnten, eine Art Jugendclub. Wir könnten viel Spaß haben, ohne viel Geld auszugeben.

I'm lucky because there is a lot to do for young people in my area. There is a sports centre where you can do sport and lots of fun activities. I usually go to the cinema, go shopping or play tennis in the park. The bad thing is that all this costs an arm and a leg and I can't afford it. It would be perfect if there was a place where young people could get together like a youth club. We could have fun without it costing a fortune.

What is there for tourists in your town?

Es gibt nicht viel Touristisches in meiner Umgebung, aber man kann leicht nach London mit dem Zug fahren um die Sehenswürdigkeiten, die Museen und Kunstgalerien zu sehen. Man kann auch Buckingham Palace besuchen, wo die Königin von England wohnt.

There aren't many tourist attractions in my area but we are lucky because you can easily go to London by train to see the sights, the museums and art galleries. You can also visit Buckingham Palace where the Queen of England lives.

What would you do for young people in your town?

Was mich am meisten aufregt ist, dass die Aktivitäten in meinem Bereich ein Vermögen kosten. Wenn ich etwas in meiner Umgebung ändern könnte, würde ich ein Jugendzentrum bauen, in dem sich junge Menschen treffen und Spaß haben könnten, ohne gleich den Gürtel enger schnallen zu müßen. Ausserdem würde ich mehr Fahrradwege bauen, weil ich Radfahren liebe und die Straßen wegen des Verkehrs viel zu gefährlich für Radfahrer sind.

What worries me most is that the activities in my area cost a fortune. If I could change something in my area, I would build a

youth centre so that young people could meet up and have fun
without having to pay through the nose for it. Also, I would put in
more cycle paths because I love cycling and the roads are too
dangerous for cyclists due to the traffic.

Town and countryside

Meiner Meinung nach, ist das Leben in der Stadt aus vielerlei
Gründen besser als das auf dem Land. Zum Beispiel kann man zum
Essen in Restaurant gehen, Filme anschauen, Einkaufen gehen
und sich mit Freunden treffen. Was mir am Besten gefällt, sind die
öffentlichen Verkehrsmittel. Ich fahre kein Auto und muss den Bus
nehmen, um meine Freunde zu besuchen. Wenn ich auf dem
Lande wohnte, könnte ich meine Freunde nicht so einfach
besuchen. Allerdings gibt es auch Vorteile des Landlebens. Es ist
ruhiger als die Stadt, es ist entspannter, und man kann in der
frischen Luft spazieren gehen. In der Stadt werden Verkehr und
Luftverschmutzung immer schlimmer.

In my opinion the city is better than the countryside for many
reasons. For example, you can eat in restaurants, watch films, go
shopping and meet up with friends. What I like most is the public
transport because I don't drive and I have to take the bus to go
and see my friends. If I lived in the countryside I wouldn't be able
to see my friends so easily. However, there are advantages of
living in the countryside. It is quieter than the city, it's more
relaxing and you can walk in the fresh air. In the city the traffic
and air pollution which are getting worse.

Where will you live in the future?

Wenn ich älter bin, möchte ich in London wohnen, damit ich an den Aktivitäten teilnehmen kann und in der Nähe meiner Freunden bleibe. Ich werde in einem modernen, großen, gut ausgestatteten Haus mit schöner Aussicht leben. Es ist mir wichtig, genug Platz zu haben um Parties zu feiern, weil ich so gerne tanze.

When I'm older I would like to continue living in London so I can make the most of all the activities and stay close to my friends. I will live in a modern, large, well-appointed house with pretty views. It is important that there is enough space to have parties because I love dancing.

Weather in your region today

Heute ist das Wetter gut, aber es könnte später heftig regnen. Mal sehen.

Today the weather is good but it might pour with rain later. We shall see.

Seasonal changes in your region

Im Winter ist es kälter als im Sommer, aber durch die Klimaveränderung schneit es im Winter weniger als früher. Der Unterschied zwischen den Jahreszeiten wird durch die globale Erderwärmung immer geringer.

In winter it is colder than in summer, but the climate is changing and it no longer snows in winter as it used to. The difference between the seasons is diminishing due to global warming.

Climate comparison with Germany

Das Wetter in England ist dem Wetter in Deutschland ähnlich. Daher fahren die Engländer lieber in wärmere Länder wie Spanien und Italien auf Urlaub.

The weather in England is similar to the weather in Germany. Hence the English people prefer to go on holiday to warmer countries like Spain and Italy.

Climate change in your region

Das Klima ändert sich - da gibt es gar keinen Zweifel! Autos und Flugzeuge emittieren giftige Gase, die in die Atmosphäre eindringen und die globale Erderwärmung und den Treibhauseffekt verursachen. Die Meeresspiegel steigen und es gibt Inseln, die zu verschwinden beginnen. Es gibt mehr Überschwemmungen und Stürme als je zuvor. Wir müßen handeln, bevor es zu spät ist, den Planeten zu retten.

The climate is changing – there's no doubt about it. Cars and planes emit toxic gases which go up into the atmosphere and cause global warming and the greenhouse effect. The sea levels are rising and there are islands which are beginning to disappear. There are more floods and more storms than before. We need to act before it's too late to save the planet.

Climate change solution

Wir müßen so schnell wie möglich handeln, um den Planeten zu retten. Wir sollen Fahrräder verwenden, anstatt des Autos, weniger mit dem Flugzeug reisen und Energie sparen, damit sich die natürlichen Ressourcen nicht erschöpfen. Wir sollten die Zerstörung der Tropenwälder stoppen, weil sie den Sauerstoff produzieren den wir brauchen. Wir sollten aufhören, so viel Fleisch zu essen, weil Kühe, genauso wie Autos, giftige Gase freisetzen, die den Klimawandel verursachen.

We need to act as soon as possible to save the planet. We need to use bikes instead of the car, travel less by plane and save energy so that natural resources don't run out. We should stop the destruction of tropical forests which produce the oxygen we need. We should stop eating so much meat because the cows, just like the cars, give off toxic gases which cause climate change.

Transport in your region

Ich habe Glück, dass es ein gutes öffentliches Verkehrsnetz in meiner Gegend gibt. Es gibt Züge, Busse und U-Bahnen mit denen man sehr beweglich ist. Der einzige Nachteil ist, dass der Geräuschpegel auf den Straßen sehr hoch ist und es zu viele Staus gibt. Ich glaube, wenn es mehr Radwege gäbe, hätten wir nicht so viel Luftverschmutzung.

I'm lucky because there is a good public transport network in my area. There are trains, buses and the underground and you can get around easily. The only thing is that the streets are noisy and there are too many traffic jams. If there were more cycle paths I think there wouldn't be so much air pollution.

Favourite transport

Mein Lieblingstransportmittel ist das Flugzeug, trotz der Umweltschädlichkeit, weil es schnell und komfortabel ist und man während des Fluges Filme sehen, essen, trinken und lesen kann. Ich mag Züge nicht, weil ich nie einen Platz finden kann. Wie nervig!

My favourite transport is the plane, although it is bad for the environment, because it's fast, comfortable and you can watch films, eat, drink and read during the journey. I don't like trains because I never find a seat. How annoying!

EDUCATION AND WORK

Describe your school

Meine Schule heißt .... und sie ist in .... in der
Nähe von .... Ich bin glücklich, weil es die beste
Schule der Welt ist und ich bin seit 5 Jahren dort. Was mir am
meisten gefällt, ist, dass sie sehr groß ist, mit einigen alten Teilen
und einigen modernen Teilen. Es gibt Klassenräume, Labore, ein
Esszimmer und einen Sportplatz, aber es gibt kein Schwimmbad.
Wenn es ein Schwimmbad und ein Kino gäbe, wäre es perfekt.

My school is called .... and it is in .... near
.... I'm lucky because it's the best school in the world
and I've been going there for 5 years. What I like most is that it's
big with some old parts and some modern parts. There are
classrooms, laboratories, a dining room and a sports field but
there isn't a pool. If there was a pool and a cinema it would be
perfect.

Likes and dislikes about school

Ich mag meine Schule, weil ich viele Freunde habe, aber was ich
nicht mag, ist, dass die Lehrer uns zu viel Hausaufgaben geben.
Auch wenn es einen Pool / ein Kino gäbe, würde ich mich sehr
freuen. Wenn ich etwas ändern könnte, würde ich die Uniform
ändern, weil sie unangenehm und häßlich ist. Ich habe sie satt.

I like my school because I have lots of friends but what I don't like
is that the teachers give us too much homework. Also if there was

a pool / a cinema I would be very happy. If I could change
something I would change the uniform because it's uncomfortable
and ugly. I'm sick of it.

School day

Der Unterricht beginnt um 9 Uhr und die Schule ist um 4 Uhr aus.
Wir haben sechs Unterrichtsstunden pro Tag und jeder dauert
eine Stunde. In der Pause, spiele ich mit meinen Freunden und
esse ein Sandwich. Zur Mittagszeit, gehe ich oft in einen Club.
Manchmal gehe ich zur Schule zu Fuß, aber normalerweise fahre
ich mit dem Auto und komme mit dem Zug zurück.

Lessons begin at 9 and school finishes at 4. We have 6 lessons a
day and each one lasts an hour. During break time I play with my
friends and eat a sandwich. I often go to a club at lunchtime.
Sometimes I walk to school but normally I go to school by car and
come back by train. I usually do two hours of homework in the
evening.

Subjects

Ich studiere Französisch, Spanisch, Kunst, Latein, Englisch, Sport,
Naturwissenschaften, Mathematik, Musik, Geschichte und
Geographie. Mein Lieblingsfach ist ... .. weil der Lehrer schön ist
und ich gute Noten bekomme. Ich mag Latein nicht, weil es
schwierig ist, weil der Lehrer langweilig ist und er uns zu viele
Hausaufgaben gibt.

I am studying French, Spanish, art, Latin, English, sport, sciences, maths, music, history and geography. My favourite subject is ….. because the teacher is nice and I get good marks. I don't like Latin because it's difficult, the teacher is boring and the teacher gives us too much homework.

Describe a teacher

Mein Deutschlehrer ist natürlich mein Lieblingslehrer. Er / sie heißt ………… .. und er / sie hat blonde Haare und blaue Augen. Was ich am meisten mag ist, dass er der intelligenteste Lehrer in der Schule ist, mich zum Lachen bringt und gleichzeitig immer alles sehr langsam erklärt, so dass ich verstehe, was wir tun.

My German teacher is my favourite teacher of course. He / she is called …………. and he / she has blonde hair and blue eyes. What I like most is that he / she is the most intelligent teacher in the school, makes me laugh and at the same time always explains everything very slowly so I can understand what we are doing.

Describe your uniform

Wir müßen eine Uniform tragen - einen schwarzen Rock, ein weißes Hemd, eine schwarze Hose, eine schwarze Jacke, schwarze Schuhe, Socken oder Strumpfhosen, eine Krawatte und einen Pullover. Wenn ich etwas ändern könnte, würde ich die Uniform ändern, weil sie unangenehm und häßlich ist. Ich habe sie satt.

We have to wear a uniform – [a black skirt, a white shirt, black trousers, a black jacket, black shoes, socks or tights, a tie and a jumper]. If I could change something I would change the uniform because it's uncomfortable and ugly. I'm sick of it.

Opinion of uniform

Natürlich gibt es Vorteile des Uniformtragens. Man muss nicht darüber nachdenken, was man am Morgen anziehen wird und es gibt keinen Druck, sich modisch zu bekleiden. Jeder sieht gleich aus und auf diese Weise kann man Stier in den Schulen vermeiden. Wenn ich etwas ändern könnte, würde ich die Uniform ändern, weil sie unangenehm und häßlich ist. Ich habe sie satt.

Of course there are advantages to wearing a uniform. You don't have to think about what you are going to wear in the morning and there is no pressure to dress in a fashionable way. Everyone looks the same and in this way you can avoid bulling in schools. If I could change something I would change the uniform because it's uncomfortable and ugly. I'm sick of it.

Yesterday at school

Gestern bin ich mit dem Bus zur Schule gegangen und als ich ankam, habe ich mit meinen Freunden geplaudert. Der Unterricht hat um 9 Uhr angefangen und ich habe 5 Klassen von 40 Minuten vor dem Mittagessen gehabt. In der Pause um 10.20 habe ich einen Keks gegessen und Basketball gespielt. Während der Mittagspause haben wir in der Kantine gegessen und danach bin ich zum Drama-Club gegangen, weil es mein Lieblingshobby ist. Die Schule war um 4 Uhr aus und ich bin nach Hause gegangen, um Abend zu essen und meine Hausaufgaben zu machen.

Yesterday I went to school by bus and when I arrived I chatted with my friends. Lessons began at 9 and I had 5 classes of 40 minutes each before lunch. During break at 10.20 I ate a biscuit and played basketball. During the lunch hour we ate in the canteen and afterwards I went to drama club because it's my favourite hobby. Lessons finished at 4 and I went home to have dinner and do my homework.

Opinion of homework

Obwohl es nützlich ist, um den Klassenunterricht besser zu verstehen, ärgern mich die Hausaufgaben, weil die Lehrer uns zu viele geben. Ich habe zwei Stunden Hausaufgaben pro Tag und ich bin immer erschöpft! Wenn wir keine Hausaufgaben hätten, zumindest während der Woche, wäre es viel besser.

Although it's useful for understanding what we have learnt in class, homework annoys me because the teachers give us too much. I have two hours of homework per day and I'm always exhausted! If we didn't have any, at least during the week, it would be much better.

What you'd change at school

Wenn ich etwas ändern könnte, würde ich die Uniform ändern, weil sie unangenehm und häßlich ist. Ich habe sie satt. Es wäre auch besser, wenn es während der Woche keine Hausaufgaben gäbe. Das Wichtigste ist, dass die Schüler in der Klasse wach sind, so dass sie studieren und lernen können. Es wäre noch besser, wenn der Unterricht später anfangen würde, weil nach Ansicht der Wissenschaftler, brauchen junge Menschen mehr Schlaf am Morgen.

If I could change something I would change the uniform because it's uncomfortable and ugly. I'm sick of it. It would also be better if there wasn't any homework during the week. The important thing is that students are wide awake in class so that they can study and learn. It would even better if lessons began later because, according to scientists, young people need more sleep in the morning.

School rules

Die Regeln sind sehr streng. So kann man das Handy während des Unterrichts nicht benutzen; man kann auch kein Kaugummi kauen. Wenn wir plaudern, werden die Lehrer gekreuzigt. Gestern habe ich eine Haftverpflichtung zum Unterricht erhalten und musste bis 17 Uhr in der Schule bleiben. Das Make-up ist nicht erlaubt, aber die Mädchen tragen es trotzdem.

The rules are quite strict. For example, you can't use your phone during lessons; you can't chew gum either. If we chat, the teachers

get cross. Yesterday I got a detention for talking in class and had
to stay at school until 5pm. Make-up isn't allowed but the girls
wear it anyway.

Ideal school

Meine ideale Schule wäre groß und modern und würde in der
Nähe meines Hauses liegen. Sie würde ein Sportzentrum
einschliessen, wo wir viele Stunden Basketball spielen würden, ein
riesiges Schwimmbad und ein Kino, wo wir uns stundenlang
enstspannen würden. Es gäbe keine Uniform und die Lehrer
würden keine Hausaufgaben geben. Der Unterricht würde am
Mittag beginnen, denn nach Ansicht der Wissenschaftler
brauchen wir mehr Schlaf am Morgen. Wie hervorragend!

My ideal school would be big and modern and would be near my
house. There would be a sports centre where we would spend
many hours playing basketball, an enormous pool and a cinema
where we would relax four hours on end. There wouldn't be a
uniform and the teachers wouldn't give homework. Lessons would
begin at midday because according to scientists, young people
need more sleep in the morning. How perfect!

Primary school

Als ich jung war, war ich in einer Grundschule neben meinem
Haus. Die Lehrer waren nett und gaben uns nicht so viel
Hausaufgaben wie jetzt. Wie toll! Es gab einen großen Garten, wo

wir spielten. Das Schlechte war, dass ich das Mittagessen nicht essen konnte, weil man uns zu viele Gemüse gab.

When I was Young I went to a primary school near my house. The teachers were nice and didn't give us as much homework as they do now. How great! There was a big garden where we used to play at breaktime. The bad thing was that I didn't like the school dinners because they gave us too many vegetables.

German and English schools

Es scheint, dass deutsche Schulen weniger streng als englische Schulen sind. Sie haben keine Uniform und die Atmosphäre in der Schule ist viel lockerer, weil die Schüler keine Angst vor den Lehrern haben. Mein deutscher Freund sagte mir, dass sie weniger Prüfungen haben. Wie glücklich! Ich bin so eifersüchtig auf die deutschen Studenten.

It seems that German schools are less strict than English schools. They don't have uniform and the atmosphere in the school is much nicer because the pupils are not scared of the teachers. My German friend told me that she has fewer exams. How lucky! I am so jealous of the German students.

Future education

Nächstes Jahr werde ich Englisch, Geschichte und Mathematik weitermachen, weil sie meine Lieblingsfächer sind. Ich werde Mathe und Wissenschaft aufgeben, weil sie mich langweilen. Ich

werde viel arbeiten, damit ich zu einer guten Universität gehen
kann, wo ich hoffe, Jura zu studieren.

*Next year I am going to carry on studying English, history and
maths because they are my favourite subjects. I will give up maths
and science because they bore me. I will work hard so I can go to a
good university, where I hope to study law.*

Part time job

Im letzten Jahr verbrachte ich eine Woche in einer Schule und es
hat mir gefallen, aber ich habe wie ein Gaul geschuftet und nichts
verdient. Jetzt habe ich seit zwei Monaten einen Teilzeitjob in
einem Restaurant in meiner Stadt, das Pizza Mama heißt und es
ist etwas ganz Anderes. Ich arbeite samstags von 2 bis 6 Uhr. Ich
arbeite in der Küche, ich spüle das Geschirr ab und wasche die
Gemüse und den Salat. Im Restaurant selbst lege ich die Tische
und diene die Kunden. Was mir am meisten gefällt ist das Geld,
weil die Kunden immer riesige Tipps geben. So was!

*Last year I spent a week working in a school and I liked it a lot but I
worked my socks off and earned nothing. Now I have had a part
time job for the past two months in a restaurant in my area called
Pizza Mama and it's something else entirely. I work on Saturdays
from 2 till 6. I work in the kitchen washing dishes and preparing
vegetables and salads. In the restaurant itself I lay the tables and
serve clients. What I like most is the money because the clients
always give huge tips. I love it!*

Future job

Ich weiß nicht genau, was ich tun will, wenn ich älter bin. Das Wichtigste ist, dass es interessant ist. Ich möchte Geschichtslehrer werden, weil es mein Lieblingsfach ist, und Lehrer sind glücklich, weil sie nicht während des Sommers arbeiten müßen.

I don't know exactly what I want to do when I'm older. The important thing is that it is interesting. I would like to become a history teacher because it's my favourite subject, and teachers are lucky because they don't work during the summer.

Ideal job

Wenn ich wählen könnte und wenn ich nicht Geld verdienen müßte, würde ich in ein Land der Dritten Welt fahren, um als Arzt freiwillig zu arbeiten. Es gibt Millionen von Menschen die wegen der Kriege und des Terrorismus leiden, und ich möchte etwas tun, um ihnen zu helfen.

If I could choose and if I didn't have to earn money I would go to a third world country to do voluntary work as a doctor. There are millions of people suffering because of wars and terrorism and I'd like to do something to help them.

HOLIDAYS

Usual holidays

Ich habe Glück, weil ich jedes Jahr mit meiner Familie mit dem Flugzeug nach Spanien fliege und zwei Wochen in einem Hotel in der Nähe des Strandes verbringe. Mir gefällt das sehr, weil es meiner Meinung nach das beste Land der Welt ist. Es ist heiß, die Leute sind nett und das Essen ist sehr lecker. Normalerweise entspanne ich mich stundenlang und vergesse den Stress meines Lebens. Ich spiele jeden Tag Tennis, ich sonne, schwimme im Meer und treffe neue Freunde. Das macht Spaß.

I'm lucky because every year I go to Spain by plane with my family and we stay in a hotel near the beach for two weeks. I love it because in my opinion it is the best country in the world. It's hot, the people are nice and the food is delicious. I usually spend hours relaxing and forgetting the stress of my life. I play tennis every day, I sunbathe, swim in the sea and make new friends. I have a great time.

Last year's holiday

Ich habe Glück, weil ich vor einem Jahr .....mit dem Boot / Auto / Flugzeug mit einem Freund / mit Freunden / mit meiner Familie nach .... weggefahren bin. Ich habe .... Tage / Wochen / Monate dort verbracht. Wir waren in einem Hotel in der Nähe des Strandes. Ich habe mich gesonnt, bin geritten, habe Tennis gespielt, habe im Meer geschwommen und habe Sehenswürdigkeiten besucht. Ich habe mich entspannt, Bücher gelesen, neue Leute kennengelernt, und viel geschlafen. Es war jeden Tag sonnig. Es hat viel Spaß gemacht.

I am lucky because a year ago I went to ....by boat / car / plane with a friend / with friends / with my family. I spent .... days / weeks / months there. We stayed in a hotel near the beach. I sunbathed, went horse-riding, played tennis, swam in the sea, visited historical sites, relaxed, read books, met new people, slept a lot. It was sunny every day. I had a great time.

Purchases on hoilday

Ich habe meinen besten Freund zum Geburtstag ein rotes T-Shirt gekauft. Wenn ich gekonnt hätte, hätte ich ihm etwas Interessanteres gekauft, aber ich konnte es mir nicht leisten.

I bought a red T-shirt for my best friend's birthday. If I could have I would have bought him something more interesting but I couldn't afford it.

Future holiday

Im nächsten Jahr / wenn ich meine Prüfungen beendet habe, werde ich mit meiner Familie und einigen Freunden nach Griechenland fahren. Wir werden in einem Hotel in der Nähe des Strandes wohnen und jeden Tag Tennis spielen. Ich werde sonnen, im Meer schwimmen und mich entspannen, weil ich mich nach den Prüfungen ausruhen muss. Ich freue mich darauf.

Next year / when I have finished my exams, I will go to Greece with my family and some friends. We will stay in a hotel near the beach and we are going to play tennis every day. I will sunbathe, swim in the sea and relax because I will need to rest after the exams. I am looking forward to it.

Ideal holiday

Wenn ich reich wäre, würde ich mit meinem besten Freund nach Frankreich fahren. Wir würden in einem 5-Sterne-Hotel in der Nähe des Strandes übernachten. Wir würden uns jeden Tag entspannen, Tennis spielen, im Meer schwimmen und Sonnenbaden. Wir würden neue Freunde kennenlernen, wir würden regionale Gerichten probieren und Souvenirs kaufen. Es würde jeden Tag sonnig sein. Wie perfekt!

If I was rich I would go to France with my best friend. We would stay in a five-star hotel near the beach. We would spend every day relaxing, playing tennis, swimming in the sea and sunbathing. We would make new friends, we would try the local dishes and buy souvenirs. It would be sunny every day. How perfect!

Holidays with parents or friends?

Der grte Vorteil des Urlaubs mit meinen Eltern ist, dass sie für alles bezahlen und ich selbst an nichts denken muss. Wir übernachten in Luxushotels und essen regionale Gerichte. Der Nachteil ist, dass ich Sehenswürdigkeiten besuchen muss, die mich gar nicht interessieren. Wie langweilig! Ich möchte mit meinen Freunden weggehen, damit ich die Freiheit und den Verzicht auf Museen genießen kann.

The good thing about going on holiday with my parents is that they pay for everything and I don't have to think about anything. We stay in luxury hotels and we eat local food. The bad thing is that I have to visit tourist sites which don't interest me. How boring! I would like to go on holiday with my friends so that I can make the most of the freedom and the lack of museums.

Importance of holidays

Das Urlaub ist aus vielen Gründen wichtig. Erstens müßen wir uns nach der Arbeit entspannen, wenn wir wie ein Gaul geschuftet haben. Es ist auch wichtig, die Kultur der fremden Länder kennenzulernen, damit wir ein besseres Verständnis für die anderen Menschen auf der Welt entwickeln können. Außerdem, kann man neue Sportarten erlernen und die Gelegenheit nutzen, zum ersten Mal neue Aktivitäten auszuprobieren

Holidays are important for many reasons. Firstly, we need to relax after work when we have been working our socks off. Also it's important to get to know the culture of foreign countries so that we can have a better understanding of the people of the world. Also, you can learn new sports and take the opportunity to try new activities for the first time.

MODERN WORLD AND ENVIRONMENT

Nowadays what are the biggest environmental problems?

Heutzutage, gibt es eine Menge Probleme mit der Umwelt. Ich bin über die Luftverschmutzung besonders beunruhigt. Autos, Fabrike, die Industrie – alle geben Giftstoffe ab, die die Atmosphäre verunreinigen und zur Luftverschmutzung, zur Erderwärmung und zum Treibhauseffekt führen. Folglich, steigen die Temperaturen und schmeizen die Polkappen, was alles zu einem steigenden Meeresspiegel führt. Ich mache mir für die künftigen Generationen ganz viele Sorgen wegen der Probleme der Erderwärmung.

Nowadays, there are a lot of environmental problems. I am most concerned about pollution. Cars, factories and industry emit toxic gases, which go into the atmosphere and cause air pollution, global warming and the greenhouse effect. Consequently, the temperatures increase, the polar ice caps melt and as a result of all this the sea level rises. I am afraid for the future generations due to the problems of global warming.

Why protect the environment?

Trotz unserer Bemühungen, ist unser Planet am Rande des Todes. Was für eine Katastrophe! Wenn wir nicht etwas dringend unternehmen, wird sich die Situation nur verschlechtern, also müßen wir alle für die Umwelt kämpfen. Wir können keineswegs die Probleme der Erderwärmung hinwegsetzen.

In spite of our efforts, our planet is about to die. What a disaster! If we do not do anything, the situation will only get worse, so we must all fight for the environment. It is impossible to close our eyes to the problems associated with global warming.

Recycling

Meiner Meinung nach, ist jeder Einzelner für den Schutz des Planets verantwortlich. Das Wichtigste ist irgendetwas zu tun; stets die kleinste Bemühung kann die Sache völlig ändern. In meiner Familie, versuchen wir am besten alles wiederzuverwerten; der Karton, das Papier, Flaschen, Kunststoffe, das Glas, Dosen und die Verpackung.

I believe that the protection of the planet should be everybody's responsibility. The most important thing is to act, even the smallest act can make a difference. In my family we try our best to recycle everything; cardboard, paper, bottles, plastic, glass, tins and packaging.

The importance of recycling

Heute ist die Situation mit der Umwelt sehr beunruhigend geworden. Es ist absolut erforderlich, dass wir alles Mögliche wiederverwerten, damit wir unsere Naturschätze nicht erschöpfen und wir unseren Kindern eine saubere Welt erben.

Nowadays the situation in relation to the environment is very worrying. It is essential that we recycle everything possible so our natural resources don't run out and so that we leave our children a clean world.

What do you do for the environment at home?

Ich tue, was ich kann, um die Umwelt zu sch<u>ü</u>tzen. Zum Beispiel, nehme ich Duschen statt Bäder, um das Wasser zu sparen; ich verausschalte die Lichter, um Elektrizität zu sparen und ich mache den Hahn zu, um Wasser zu bewahren. Ich nehme so oft wie möglich öffentliche Verkehrsmittel, statt mit dem Auto zu fahren, und ich kaufe umweltfreundliche Produkte.

I do what I can to protect the environment. For example, I shower instead of taking a bath to save water, I turn off the lights to save electricity and the taps when I'm not using them. Also we do our best to recycle cardboard, paper, plastic and glass. I make the most of public transport instead of travelling by car and I buy green products.

What do you do for the environment at school?

In der Schule, tun wir unser `Bestes, alles zu tun, um die Umwelt zu schützen. Es gibt in jedem Klassenzimmer einen Recyclingbehalter; wir schalten die Lichter aus, wenn wir das Klassenzimmer verlassen, um Strom zu sparen; und die Lehrer ermutigen uns, mit den öffentlichen Verkehrsmitteln statt mit dem Auto in die Schule zu gehen, weil die kleinste Tat einen Unterschied machen kann.

At school we do our best to do everything possible to protect the environment. There is a recycling bin in every classroom, we turn off the lights when we leave the classrooms to save electricity, and the teachers encourage us to use public transport instead of a car to travel to school, because the simplest act can make a difference.

What should we be doing for the environment?

Es ist wichtig, dass wir alle für die Umwelt kämpfen, so dass uns die Naturschätze nicht ausgehen und so dass unsere Kinder in einer sauberen Welt leben können. Wir sollten auch weiterhin alles Mögliche machen, weil die kleinste Tat einen Unterschied machen kann. Zum Beispiel sollten wir Duschen statt Bäder nehmen, um Wasser zu sparen; die Lichter ausschalten, wenn wir einen Raum verlassen, um Strom zu sparen; wir sollten alles Mögliche wiederverwerten und sollten öffentliche Verkehrsmittel benutzen statt mit dem Auto fahren, um die Luftverschmutzung zu reduzieren.

It is essential that we all fight for the environment so that natural resources don't run out and so that our children can live in a clean world. We should continue to do everything possible because the simplest act can make a difference. For example, we should shower instead of having baths to save water, we should turn off the lights when we leave a room to save electricity, recycle everything possible and we should make the most of public

transport instead of travelling by car in order to reduce air
pollution.

What should the government do for the environment?

Es ist ganz erforderlich, dass wir Gesetze haben, die die Umwelt schützen. Zum Beispiel, denke ich, dass die Regierung die Anzahl von Autos auf den Straßen beschränken sollte und mehr Radwege bauen sollte, damit wir mit dem Fahrrad statt mit dem Auto reisen können. Wenn es mehr Radwege gäbe, denke ich, dass es nicht so viel Luftverschmutzung geben würde.

It's fundamental that we have laws to protect the environment. For example, I think that the government should limit the number of cars on the roads and should construct more cycle routes so that we can use bicycles instead of cars. If there were more cycle routes I think that there wouldn't be as much air pollution.

The causes of poverty in the world

Was mich am meisten beunruhigt ist die Armut. Die Hälfte der Welt lebt in Armut und die andere Hälfte wirft gutes Essen weg. Die Armut wird immer mehr weitverbreitet, wegen der Kriege, dem Klimawandel und dem politischen Konflikt. Die Städte der Welt sind übervölkert und in kurzer Zeit wird es große Probleme mit dem Wohnraum geben. Weltkonflikte zwingen Millionen von Menschen vor Hunger und Verfolgung zu fliehen. Derzeit ist die Flüchtlingskrise in Europa in einem kritischen humanitären

Zustand. Sogar in England leben viele Menschen unterhalb der Armutsgrenze, und die Situation wird immer schlimmer. Es gibt viele Familien, in denen niemand für Generationen einen Job gehabt hat. Die Regierung sollte mehr tun, um die Kinder in diesen Familien zu fördern, so dass sie eine Ausbildung und andere Möglichkeiten zugreifen, die sie verdienen.

What worries me most is poverty. Half the world is living in poverty and the other half is throwing away decent food. Poverty is becoming more and more widespread because of wars, a changing climate and political conflict. The cities of the world are overpopulated, and in a short time there will be big problems with living space. World conflicts force millions of people to flee hunger and persecution. Currently the refugee crisis in Europe is a critical humanitarian situation. Even in England lots of people live below the poverty line and the situation is getting worse. There are lots of families where nobody has had a job for generations. The government should do more to encourage the children of these families so that they can access the education and the opportunities they deserve.

Importance of the news

Die Medien können einen wichtigen positiven Einfluss haben. Sie informieren uns über Aktualitäten und wir sollten uns alle über Weltergebnisse erkundigen. Was jedoch wichtig ist, ist dass die Medien unvoreingenommen sind, weil die Medien heute so mächtig sind. Es ist wichtig, dass wir Gesetze haben, damit die

Medien nicht lügen können und ihre Leser nicht manipulieren können, wie sie es in anderen Ländern der Welt tun.

The news can have a major positive influence. It informs us on current issues and we all need to know what is happening in the world. However, what is important is that the news is unbiased because the media is so powerful today. It is essential that we have laws so that the media cannot lie and manipulate its readers as they do in other countries in the world.

Do you watch the news?

Ich interessiere mich für die Nachrichten und wenn ich mehr Zeit hätte, würde ich jeden Tag die Zeitung lesen, aber die Lehrer geben uns zu viele Hausaufgaben und ich finde es schwer, auf dem Laufenden zu halten. Ich habe die BBC App auf meinem Handy, das mir sagt, wenn es in der Welt etwas Wichtiges passiert und wenn ich mehr davon wissen will, klicke ich auf das Symbol, um es zu öffnen.

I am interested in the news and if I had more time I would read a paper every day, but the teachers give us too much homework and I find it hard to stay up to date. I have the BBC app on my phone which tells me when something important happens in the world and if I want to know more, I click on the icon to open it.

What's in the news at the moment?

Was die Schlagzeilen betrifft, sind sie oft über den Terrorismus oder die Umwelt. Es ist als ob, wir uns stets in einem Kriegszustand finden, und wir wissen nicht, wann oder wo der nächste Terroranschlag geschehen wird. Darüber hinaus, werden die Umweltprobleme immer schlechter. Wegen des Klimawandels, gibt es mehr Erdbeben, Stürme und Überschwemmungen, die eine Menge Leute töten. Dazu bleibt der politische Zustand in Europa delikat, aufgrund des Anstiegs der Anti-Einwanderungsstimmung. Viele Leute denken, dass die Einwanderung verursacht den Terrorismus, weil wir die Türen für alle, auch für Verbrecher geöffnet haben. Aber zugleich müßen wir die humanitäre Krise begegnen. Wie komplex!

As far as the headlines are concerned, they are often about terrorism or the environment. It seems that we are in a permanent state of war and we don't know when or where the next terrorist attack will be. Moreover, environmental problems are getting worse. Due to climate change there are more earthquakes, storms and floods which kill a lot of people. Also, the political situation in Europe continues to be delicate due to the rise of anti-immigration feeling. Lots of people think that immigration causes terrorism because we have opened the doors to everyone, including criminals. But at the same time we need to face the humanitarian crisis. How complex!

Do you watch TV?

Sicher, ich schaue jeden Tag Seifenopern an, um zu entspannen und weil sie mich zum Lachen bringen, und ich schaue sie mit meinen Brüdern zusammen an. Ausserdem, vermisse ich nie Sport-Programme, vor allem Fußballspiele. Ich schaue von Zeit zu Zeit die Nachrichten, weil sie informativ und interessant sind. Wenn ich mehr Zeit hätte, würde ich mehr Programme anschauen, aber die Lehrer geben uns zu viele Hausaufgaben.

Yes, I watch soap operas every day to relax and because they make me laugh and I watch them together with my brothers. In addition, I never miss sports programmes, especially football matches. I watch the news from time to time because it is informative and interesting. If I had more time I would watch more programmes but the teachers give us too much homework.

Young people and TV

Ich glaube, dass wenn wir fernsehen, laufen wir dabei Gefahr, zu viel Zeit zu Hause zu verbringen. Es kann manche Leute davon abhängig machen, wobei sie keine Selbstkontrolle mehr haben, über den Anteil der Tagesstunden, den sie vor dem kleinen Bildschirm verbringen und sie wissen nicht mehr, wie sich mit Anderen zu verständigen. Ich denke jedoch, dass das Fernsehen besser als Videospiele und soziale Netzwerke ist, weil Dokumentarfilme hilfen dabei, das Bewusstsein junger Leute über soziale und globale Probleme aufzuwecken.

I believe that if we watch television we risk spending too much time stuck at home. It can create addiction in some people who lose control of the hours that they spend in front of the small screen and consequently lose the capacity to communicate face to face. However, I think that watching television is better than video games and social networks because documentaries can be an educational tool as they make young people aware of social and global problems.

Advantages of TV

Zum einen, kann Fernsehen ein pädagogisches Instrument sein, weil es viele Programme gibt, die Kindern mit dem Lernen helfen. Zum Beispiel, haben Dokumentarfilme einen positiven Einfluss, da sie uns nicht nur unterhalten, sondern uns lehren. Darüber hinaus, kann Fernsehen ein harmloses Hobby sein und die Menschen aus ihrer täglichen Routine nehmen und zur Ruhe bringen. Ich glaube, dass das Fernsehen ein guter Weg ist, nach einem anstrengenden Tag in der Schule zu entspannen.

Firstly, television can be an educational tool because there are many programmes which help children to learn. For example, documentaries have a positive influence because not only do they entertain us but also teach us. In addition, television can be a harmless hobby and can help people to rest and disconnect from their daily routine. I think that television is a good way to relax after a stressful day at school.

Disadvantages of TV

Ich glaube, dass wenn wir fernsehen, laufen wir dabei Gefahr, zu viel Zeit zu Hause zu verbringen. Manche Leute können davon abhängig werden, wobei sie keine Kontrolle mehr haben, über den Anteil der Tagesstunden, den sie vor dem kleinen Bildschirm verbringen und sie wissen nicht mehr, wie sich mit anderen zu verständigen. Außerdem, nach Ansicht vieler Menschen, gibt es im Fernsehen mehr und mehr Gewalt, vor allem in den Zeichentrickfilmen, die für Kinder gemeint sind. Wie schrecklich! Leute, die Action-Filme sehen, werden zu Gewalt desensibilisiert und Jugendliche sind nicht mehr durch schockierende Bilder betroffen.

I believe that if we watch television we risk spending too much time stuck at home. It can create addiction in some people who lose control of the hours that they spend in front of the small screen and consequently lose the capacity to communicate face to face. Also, according to many people, there is more and more violence on television, particularly in cartoons, which are aimed at children. How awful! People who watch action films are becoming desensitized to violence and young people are no longer affected by shocking images.

Advertising

Heute ist die Werbung überall um uns herum. Wohin man auch geht, sieht man Zeichen oder Anzeigen; wenn man mit dem Auto fährt, sieht man Plakaten in den Straßen und zur gleichen Zeit, hört man Anzeigen im Radio. Beim Zeitung- oder Zeitschriftlesen, findet man Anzeigen und beim Internetsurfen sieht man überall Anzeigen.

Nowadays we can see and hear advertising everywhere. Wherever you go there are signs or adverts, travelling by car we can see billboards in the streets and at the same time listen to adverts on the radio. When reading a newspaper or magazine we find adverts and while we surf the Internet we see adverts everywhere.

Positives of advertising

Der Hauptvorteil der Werbung ist, ein Produkt zum Publikum zu fördern und es ihm bekannt zu machen, und die Verbraucher über die Vorteile des Produkts zu informieren. Es ist die effektivste Methode, um die Verkäufe eines Produkts zu erhöhen, vor allem heute durch soziale Netzwerke. Zusätzlich, obwohl es lästig sein kann, ist die Werbung der Grund, warum soziale Netzwerke wie Facebook kostenlos bleiben.

The main advantage of advertising is to promote and publicise a product to the public, and to inform the consumer about the benefits of the product. It is the most effective method of increasing the sales of a product, especially today by using social networks. Also, although it can be annoying, advertising is the reason why social networks like Facebook remain free of charge.

Negatives of advertising

Die Werbung bringt uns oft dazu, Produkte oder Dienstleistungen zu kaufen und sie kann man gierig machen. Ich denke, dass die Werbung, die das Junkfood und die Zigaretten fördert, verboten werden sollte, weil sie Produkte fördert, die ungesund sind und schwere Krankheiten wie Krebs verursachen können. Die Werbung kann auch einen gefährlichen Einfluss auf junge Menschen üben, die meinen, sie sollten so dünn und attraktiv sein wie die Modelle, die sie auf den Anzeigen im Fernsehen oder wo auch immer schauen. Der Druck kann Essstörungen wie die Magersucht verursachen.

Advertising often deceives us to make us buy products or services and can provoke greed in people. I think that adverts promoting junk food and cigarettes should be banned because they promote products which are bad for your health and can cause serious illnesses like cancer. Also, advertising can have a dangerous influence on young people who think they should be as thin and gorgeous as the models they see on the adverts, on TV, wherever. The pressure can cause eating disorders like anorexia.

Cinema

Ich habe Filme und Kino gerne. Obwohl ich nicht viel Geld habe, gehe ich sonntagmorgens mit meiner älteren Schwester ins Kino. Bevor wir fortsetzen, finde ich die besten Filme im Internet. Meine Schwester mag romantische Filme, während ich Science-Fiction und Action-Filme bevorzuge. Wenn ich mehr Geld hätte, würde ich jeden Tag gehen, aber es ist sehr kostspielig, und ich kann es mir nicht leisten.

I like films and cinema. On Sunday mornings, although I don't have much money, I go to the cinema with my older sister. Before going I find the best films on the Internet. My sister likes romantic films whilst I prefer science fiction and action films. If I had more money, I'd go every day but it costs an arm and a leg and I can't afford it.

What films do you like?

Was das Kino betreibt, mag ich überhaupt keine romantischen Filme. Ich bevorzuge Action-Filme, vor allem James-Bond-Filme, weil sie spannend sind, und mich nicht langweilen. Es gibt bei jenen Filmen eine Menge Spezialeffekte und viele Filmstars. Normalerweise, gehe ich jedes Wochenende mit meinen Freunden ins Kino. Wenn ich mehr Geld hätte, würde ich jeden Tag gehen, aber es ist sehr kostspielig, und ich kann es mir nicht leisten.

As for cinema, I do not like romantic films at all. I prefer action films, above all James Bond films because they are exciting and they don't bore me. There are loads of special effects and lots of movie stars acting in them. I usually go to the cinema every weekend with my friends. If I had more money, I'd go every day but it costs an arm and a leg and I can't afford it.

Cinema or TV?

Ich gehe lieber ins Kino, denn ich mag Science-Fiction-Filme sehr, und ich finde es ganz toll, sie auf der großen Leinwand zu schauen. Ich genieße dabei viel mehr die Effekte, den Soundtrack und die visuellen Effekte. Auch wenn mann ein Film zu Hause schaut, gibt es viele Ablenkungen, und es gibt immer jemanden, der das Kanal wechseln will.

I prefer the cinema because I love science fiction films and I prefer to watch them on the big screen. I enjoy the effects, the soundtrack and the visual effects much more. Also when you watch a film at home there are loads of distractions and there is always someone who wants to change channel.

The last film you saw

Ich habe gerade den Film *Titanic* angesehen und es war großartig. Es handelt sich um zwei junge Liebende, deren Schicksale auf der Jungfernfahrt des Kreuzfahrtschiffes *Titanic* kreuzten. Wenn aber das Schiff einen Eisberg im gefrorenen Nordatlantik trifft, verwandelt ihre leidenschaftliche Begegnung in einen verzweifelten Wettlauf zum Überleben. Es überrascht mich kaum, dass es der erfolgreichste Film aller Zeiten ist.

I have just watched Titanic and it was great. It is about two young lovers whose destinies cross on the inaugural journey of the cruise ship Titanic. But when the ship hits an iceberg in the frozen North Atlantic their passionate encounter becomes a desperate race to survive. It doesn't surprise me that it's the most successful film of all time.

Mobile phones – do you have one and why?

Ich habe Glück, denn ich habe schon seit fünf Jahren mein eigenes Handy, und ich verwende es, Nachrichten zu senden, mit meinen Freunden auf soziale Netzwerken zu reden, Fotos zu machen, Musik zu hören und ins Internet zu gehen. Was ich am meisten mag, ist, dass Handys die Kommunikation wesentlich erleichtert haben; immerhin, wenn ich es mir leisten könnte, würde ich das neueste Modell kaufen, weil mein Handy veraltet ist. Ich könnte ohne mein Handy nicht überleben. Ich bin davon ganz abhängig.

I am lucky because I have had my own mobile for 5 years and I use it to send messages, talk to my friends on social networks, listen to music, take photos and go on the internet. What I like most is that mobiles make communication much easier but if I had more money, I would buy the latest model because my mobile is out-dated. I could not survive without my phone. I am addicted to it.

Young people and mobile phones

Junge Leute haben Handys sehr gerne, weil sie extrem nützlich sind, um mit Freunden in sozialen Netzwerken Chats zu machen, Musik herunterzuladen und zu hören, Fotos zu machen und im Internet zu surfen. Für die meisten junge Leute ist ein Leben ohne Handy unvorstellbar und ihre Sucht kann gefährlich sein.

Young people like mobile phones because they are extremely useful, to chat to friends on social networks, download and listen to music, take photos and surf the web. Most young people couldn't manage without a mobile and their addiction can be dangerous.

Advantages of technology

1. Es gibt keinen Zweifel daran, dass Mobiltelefone die Kommunikation erleichtert haben. Der Hauptvorteil ist, dass man mit Menschen auf der ganzen Welt kommunizieren kann.

    There is no doubt that mobile phones make communication much easier. The main advantage is that you can communicate with people all over the world.

2. Wir können über alles herausfinden, wann immer wir wollen. Es hilft mir bei meinen Hausaufgaben.

    We can find out about anything whenever we like. It helps me with my homework.

3. Die Technologie ermöglicht mich, mit allen in Kontakt zu bleiben, und ich ziehe den größten Nutzen aus Apps wie WhatsApp und Snapchat, um mit meinen Freunden die ganze Zeit zu kommunizieren.

    Technology allows me to stay in contact with everyone and I make the most of apps like Whatsapp and Snapchat to communicate with my friends all the time.

4. Ich halte mich auf dem Laufenden dank der Nachrichten-Apps, die mich wissen lassen, wenn es etwas Wichtiges passiert.

    I stay up to date using the news apps which let me know when something important happens

5. Man kann Filme und Musik herunterladen. Normalerweise höre ich auf mein Telefon die ganze Zeit Musik und es macht die Reise in die Schule viel lustiger. Wie glücklich sind wir! Es gibt keine Grenzen.

    You can download films and music. I usually spend a lot of time listening to music on my phone and it makes the journey to school much more fun. How lucky we are! There are no limits.

Disadvantages of technology

1. Was mich am meisten beunruhigt ist, dass junge Leute heute um ihre Geräte geklebten bleiben und man kann davon abhängig sein. Man weiß nicht mehr, wie sie mit anderen umgehen sollen, und das Ergebnis ist, dass die Schüler weniger danach streben, ihre Hausaufgaben zu machen, weil sie abgelenkt sind, und sie werden einsam und traurig.
    What worries me most is that nowadays, young people stay glued to their devices and you can become addicted. They lose the capacity to communicate face to face and the result is that students strive less to do their homework because they are distracted and they become lonely and sad.

2. Wir sind stets nach unseren Geräten so süchtig, dass wir Unfälle riskieren, wenn wir fahren oder die Straßen überqueren.

   We are getting so addicted to our devices that we risk having accidents when we are driving or crossing the road.

3. Darüber hinaus, wenn man eine Nachricht elektronisch sendet, erwartet man eine sofortige Antwort, so dass der Druck zum Stress und zu anderen gesundheitlichen Probleme führen kann.

   In addition, if you send a message electronically, you expect an immediate answer so that pressure can cause stress and other health problems.

4. Es besteht immer das Risiko, dass unsere Computer sich von einem Virus infizieren und unsere Privatdaten missgebraucht werden, und wir laufen die Gefahr, Opfer von Cyber-Kriminalität zu werden.

   There are always risks of viruses infecting our computers and private information can be misused and we risk being victims of cybercrime.

5. Ein weiteres Risiko, das von der Internetnutzung stammt, ist der Kontakt mit Fremden, vor allem für junge Menschen. Gefährliche Menschen können sich hinter dem Bildschirm verstecken und eine falsche Identität verwenden, so dass wir eigentlich nicht richtig wissen, mit wem wir uns unterhalten. Zum Beispiel, sah ich gestern die Nachrichten, und sie sprach von einem 16-jährigen Mädchen, das ihren "Freund" auf

Facebook kennengelernt hatte, aber in Wirklichkeit war er ein alter Mann und leider hat er sie getötet. Wie schockierend!

Another risk of Internet use is being in contact with strangers, especially for young people. Dangerous people can hide behind the screen and use false identities so that we don't know who we are really speaking too. For example, yesterday I saw the news and they spoke about a 16 year- old girl who met her 'boyfriend' on Facebook, but in reality he was an old man and unfortunately he killed her. How shocking!

The future of mobile phones

In die Zukunft, glaube ich, dass Handys dünner, mit größeren Bildschirmen und nützlicher werden werden. Aber was auch immer passiert, werden sie kräftiger sein, und wir werden ganz vorsichtig dabei sein müßen, wie wir Informationen im Internet weitergeben, wegen des Risikos, dass wir Opfer von Cyber-Kriminalität werden.

In the future, I believe that mobiles will become thinner with bigger screens and more useful. But whatever happens they will be more powerful and we will have to be careful with the information we share on the internet because we risk being victims of cybercrime.

SOCIAL ACTIVITIES, FITNESS AND HEALTH

What do you eat on a normal day?

Jeden Morgen, esse ich Müsli, weil es eine Energiequelle ist und das hilft mir beim Lernen. In der Schule, esse ich ein Sandwich und ein Stück Obst, obwhol wenn ich könnte, würde ich Fisch und Chips essen. Wenn ich wieder nach Hause komme, esse ich immer Schokolade, obwohl es nicht gesund ist, weil ich davon abhängig bin, und es macht mir das Wasser im Mund. Zum Abendessen esse ich Fleisch mit Gemüse, Pasta, Huhn oder Pizza. Ich sollte weniger Schokolade und mehr Obst und Gemüse essen, um Herzprobleme zu vermeiden.

Every morning I eat cereal because it is a source of energy and this helps me when I work. I eat a sandwich and fruit at school but if I had the chance I would like to eat fish and chips. On returning home, I always eat chocolate although it is bad for you, because I am addicted and it makes my mouth water. I eat meat and vegetables, pasta, chicken or pizza for dinner. I should eat less chocolate and more fruit and vegetables in order to avoid heart problems.

General eating habits

Ich versuche, gesund zu essen, obwohl es manchmal sehr schwierig ist. Ich esse 5 Portionen Obst und Gemüse pro Tag, und ich vermeide Zucker. Es ist manchmal schwierig, weil Schokolade und Süßigkeiten schmecken mir sehr, aber ich denke, es ist okay, ungesunde Dinge in Maßen zu sich nehmen. Als ich jung war, wollte ich nicht jeden Tag gesund essen und jeden Tag bat ich um Fast-Food. Mein Lieblingsessen war Chips und ich wollte nichts anders essen.

I try to eat healthily although it is quite difficult sometimes. I eat 5 portions of fruit and vegetables per day and I avoid sugar. It's hard sometimes because I love eating chocolate and sweet things but I think it's okay to have unhealthy things in moderation. When I was young I used to hate healthy food and every day I asked for fast food. My favourite food was chips and I didn't want to eat anything else.

What don't you like eating?

In der Regel esse ich alles, aber wenn ich ein Lebensmittel unbedingt wählen müßte, das mir nicht besonders schmeckt, wäre es Spargel.

I usually eat everything, but if I had to choose a type of food that I don't like very much, it would be asparagus.

Lunch at school

Mittags esse ich in der Kantine, wo ich in der Regel ein Hühnchen-Sandwich oder einen Salat nehme. Zum Glück, hat sich das Schulessen im Laufe der Jahre verbessert, im Geschmack und in der Ernährung. Wie glücklich sind wir!

I eat lunch in the canteen where I usually have a chicken sandwich or a salad. Fortunately, school lunches have improved throughout the years, in flavour and in nutrition. How lucky we are!

Favourite food

Mein Lieblingsessen ist Schokolade, obwohl nicht gesund ist, weil es köstlich ist und macht mir das Wasser im Mund. Ich esse jeden Tag nach der Schule Schokolade, so dass ich die Energie habe, meine Hausaufgaben zu machen.

My favourite food is chocolate although it is bad for my health because it is delicious and makes my mouth water. I eat chocolate every day after school so that I have the energy I need to do my homework.

How to stay healthy

Um ein gesundes Leben zu führen, muss man eine abwechslungsreiche Ernährung mit fünf Portionen Obst und Gemüse pro Tag essen, weil sie uns wichtige Vitamine ergeben. Wir sollten Junk-Food vermeiden, weil es zu viel Zucker und Fett enthält und verursacht Fettleibigkeit. Darüber hinaus ist es wichtig, Sport zu treiben, Alkohol zu vermeiden und nicht zu rauchen, weil diese letzten schwere Krankheiten verursachen können. Immerhin, meine ich, dass man ungesunde Lebensmittel in Maßen essen kann.

In order to lead a healthy life, we must eat a varied diet with five portions of fruit and vegetables a day because they give us important vitamins. We should avoid junk food because it contains too much sugar and fat and causes obesity. In addition, it is important to do sport, avoid alcohol and not smoke because it can cause serious illnesses. However, I think that you can eat unhealthy food in moderation.

How you stay healthy

Um in Form zu bleiben, muss ich Sport mindestens drei Mal pro Woche in der frischen Luft treiben, zwei Liter Wasser pro Tag trinken, und ich esse fünf Portionen Obst oder Gemüse. Ich habe nie geraucht, und habe nie Drogen genommen. Ich versuche immer, Junk-Food und fetthaltige Lebensmittel zu vermeiden, obwohl es schwierig ist, weil ich der Schokolade verfallen bin, und ich versuche, mindestens acht Stunden pro Nacht zu schlafen.

In order to keep in shape, I do sport at least three times a week in the fresh air, I drink two litres of water a day and I have 5 portions of fruit or vegetables. I never smoke and I have never taken drugs. I always try to avoid junk and fatty foods, although it is difficult because I can't manage without chocolate, and I try to sleep eight hours minimum every night.

Do you like sport?

Ja, ich mag den Sport sehr. Es ist mein Lieblingsfach in der Schule, weil es einfach ist, und der Lehrer ist lustig. Was mir am meisten gefällt, ist an der frischen Luft zu sein. Nach einer Stunde Tennis fühle ich mich sehr entspannt. Normalerweise, spiele ich dreimal in der Woche Tennis und samstags mag ich die günstigen Wetterbedingungen ausschöpfen und mit meinem Vater Radfahren gehen. Wenn ich aufwachse, werde auf Sport weitermachen um mich fit zu halten und glücklich bleiben.

Yes, I like sport a lot. It is my favourite subject at school because it is easy and the teacher is fun. What I like the most is being in the fresh air. After an hour of tennis I feel very relaxed. I usually play tennis three times a week and on Saturdays I love to make the most of the good weather and go cycling with my father. When I grow up I'm going to carry on doing sport to keep fit and stay happy.

Why should we do sport?

Man sollte Sport treiben, weil es ein guter Weg ist, die Stimmung zu verbessern, den Stress abzubauen und sich fit zu halten. Man kann auch neue Freundschafte knüpfen und sein Selbstvertrauen verbessern. Wenn man Kein Sport treiben würde, würden wir die Gefahr laufen, dick zu werden, und die Fettleibigkeit kann schwere Krankheiten verursachen.

We should do sport because it is a great way to improve the mood, reduce stress and keep fit. You can also make new friends

and improve your self-confidence. If we didn't do sport, we would
risk getting fat and obesity can cause serious illnesses.

Todays' health problems

Es gibt in meinem Land eine Menge von gesundheitlichen
Problemen. Was mich am meisten beunruhigt ist die
Fettleibigkeit. Man sagt, dass fast die Hälfte der britischen Kinder
fettleibig sind. Sie verbringen zu viel Zeit vor dem Fernseher oder
um ihre Handys geklebt und sie bewegen sich nicht. Dazu essen
sie Junkfood, weil es billig, schmackhaft und einfach zu erreichen
ist. Es enthält viel Fett, Salz und Zucker, und diese können
Krankheiten wie Herzkrankheiten verursachen.

There are loads of health problems in my country. What worries
me most is obesity. It is said that almost half of British children are
obese. They spend too much time in front of the television or glued
to their mobiles and don't exercise. Also they eat junk food
because it is cheap, tasty and easy to get. It contains lots of fat,
salt and sugar and this can cause illness like heart disease.

.

The solution to health problems

Es ist notwendig, dass wir etwas tun, um die Situation zu
verbessern. Wenn ich Sportminister wäre, würde ich eine
Kampagne starten, um Kinder über die Vorteile des Sports zu
lehren. Es wäre toll, wenn es einige Prominente wären, die die
Jugendlichen bewunderten, und die ihren Lebensstil zu ändern

motivieren könnte. Es ist auch wichtig, dass es Sportzentren überall gibt, damit den jungen Leuten Sport leicht zugänglich ist. Sie existieren bereits, aber man muss Mitglied sein, und es ist teuer, deshalb können es sich junge Leute nicht leisten. Darüber hinaus, sollten gesunde Lebensmittel billiger sein.

It is necessary that we do something to improve the situation. If I were minister of sport I would launch a campaign to teach children about the benefits of sport. It would be great if there were some celebrities who young people admired that could motivate them to change their lifestyle. Also, it is essential that there are sports centres everywhere so that young people can access sport easily. They already exist but you have to be a member and it is expensive, therefore young people can't afford it. In addition, healthy food should be cheaper.

Sickness

Ich habe Glück, denn ich bin so gut wie nie krank. Normalerweise, wenn es nicht ernst ist, muss man im Bett bleiben, aber wenn man sich nach ein paar Tagen nicht besser fühlt, muss man zum Arzt. Man kann Krankheiten vermeiden, dadurch dass man einen gesunden Lebensstil führt.

I am lucky because I am almost never sick. Normally, if it is not serious you have to stay in bed but if you do not feel better after a few days, you have to go to the doctor. We can avoid illnesses by living a healthy lifestyle.

Smoking

Meiner Meinung nach ist das Rauchen lächerlich, weil jeder weiß, dass es schwere Krankheiten wie Krebs und chronische Bronchitis verursacht. Ich werde nie rauchen. Ich denke, dass heute junge Leute aus einer Menge Gründen rauchen, aber das wichtigste ist, der Gruppendruck. Wenn man auf eine Party geht, und es viele Leute gibt, die rauchen, entsteht die Versuchung, das gleiche zu machen, um sich als Teil der Gruppe zu fühlen.

In my opinion, smoking is ridiculous because everyone knows that it causes serious illnesses like cancer and chronic bronchitis. I will never smoke. I think that young people today smoke for loads of reasons, but the most important is peer pressure. If you go to a party and there are lots of people smoking, there is the temptation to do the same to feel part of the group.

Alcohol

Meiner Meinung nach ist der übermäßige Konsum von Alkohol lächerlich, weil jeder weiß, dass es schwere Krankheiten wie Leberzirrhose und Krebs verursacht. Ich werde nie übermäßig trinken. Ich denke, dass junge Leute heute Alkohol aus einer Menge Gründen trinken, aber das wichtigste ist, der Gruppendruck. Es fehlt ihnen an Selbstvertrauen und sie wenden sich an Alkohol, um tapferer zu fühlen. Wenn Sie auf eine Party gehen, und es viele betrunkene Leute gibt, entsteht die Versuchung, das gleiche zu tun.

In my opinion, the excessive consumption of alcohol is ridiculous because everyone knows that it causes serious illnesses like cirrhosis of the liver and cancer. I will never drink excessively. I think that young people today drink alcohol for loads of reasons, but the most important is peer pressure. They lack self-confidence and turn to alcohol to feel braver. If you go to a party and there are lots of drunk people, there is the temptation to do the same.

Drugs

Meiner Meinung nach, Drogen zu nehmen ist lächerlich, weil jeder weiß, dass sie schwere Krankheiten wie Panikattacken verursachen und die Funktion des Gehirns verändern kann. Ich werde nie Drogen nehmen. Ich denke, dass junge Leute heute aus mehreren Gründen Drogen nehmen, aber das wichtigste ist, der Gruppendruck. Es fehlt ihnen an Selbstvertrauen und sie wenden sich an Drogen, um tapferer zu fühlen. Wenn man auf eine Party geht, und es viele Leute gibt, die Drogen nehmen, entsteht die Versuchung, das gleiche zu tun.

In my opinion, taking drugs is ridiculous because everyone knows that they cause serious illnesses like panic attacks and can alter brain function. I will never take drugs. I think that young people today take drugs for loads of reasons, but the most important is peer pressure. They lack self-confidence and turn to drugs to feel braver. If you go to a party and there are lots of people taking drugs, there is the temptation to do the same.

Vegetarianism

Es gibt viele Gründe für den Vegetarismus. Nicht nur wollen sie keine Tiere töten, sondern haben sie auch Gründe in Bezug auf die Gesundheit und die Umwelt. Einige sagen, dass der übermäßige Konsum von Fleisch ungesund ist und zusätzlich, dass die Produktion von Fleisch die Tropenwälder und die Umwelt zerstört.

There are many reasons for vegetarianism. Not only do they not want to kill animals but also they have reasons in relation to health and the environment. Some say that eating meat excessively is bad for your health and in addition the production of meat destroys tropical forests and the environment.

Hobbies when you were young

Als ich jung war habe ich etwas weniger Sport getrieben, aber ich verbrachte den Großteil meiner Zeit im Park in der Nähe von meinem Haus, mit Freunden spielen, also habe ich die Form gehalten, ohne mich dazu zu bemühen. Außerdem, sah ich jeden Tag den fern und spielte Videospiele. Früher habe ich auch viel gelesen.

When I was young I did slightly less sport but I spent the majority of my time in the park near my house, playing with friends so I kept in shape without making an effort. Also, I watched the television every day and played videogames. I used to read a lot as well.

Ideal weekend

Mein ideales Wochenende wäre mit meiner Familie und meinen Freunden verbracht. Wenn ich wählen könnte, würde ich nach London fahren, um eine Show mit meiner Mutter zu sehen und bei der Rückkehr nach Hause würden wir Pizza essen. Wenn es möglich wäre, würden wir den folgenden Tag beim Schwimmen und Kartenspielen verbringen. Wie entspannend!

My ideal weekend would be with my family and my friends. If I could choose, I would go to London to watch a show with my mum and on returning home we would eat pizza. If it was possible we would spend the following day swimming and playing cards. How relaxing!

Books you've read

Wenn ich mit meinen Hausaufgaben fertig bin, will ich immer lesen, denn es hilft mir, mich zu entspannen. Ohne Zweifel ist mein Lieblingsbuch "Harry Potter und der Stein der Weisen", welches ich gerade zum zweiten Mal gelesen habe. Es handelt sich um Hogwarts Schule für Hexerei und Zauberei, wo Harry andere Kinder kennenlernt, die besondere Kräfte haben und er lernt alles, was notwendig ist, um Zauberer zu sein. Für mich ist das Wichtigste über das Lesen, den Stress des wirklichen Lebens zu entkommen.

When I finish my homework, I always want to read because it helps me to relax. Without a doubt my favourite book is "Harry Potter and the Philosopher's Stone" which I have just read for the second time. It is about Hogwarts school of Witchcraft and Wizardry where Harry gets to know other children who have special powers and learns everything necessary to be a wizard. For me the important thing about reading is to escape the stress of real life.

Music and musicians

Ich spiele kein Instrument, aber ich mag Musik gerne. Erstens, mag ich elektronische Musik, denn sie ist lebendig und energisch. Wenn ich ins Fitnessstudio gehe, höre ich es, damit ich schneller laufe. Die Musik hilft mir auch, mich zu enstpannen, zum Beispiel nach einem anstrengenden Tag in der Schule, was ich am meisten mag, ist mein Lieblingskünstler Ed Sheeran zu hören. Ich will ihn live sehen, aber zuerst muss ich meine Aufgaben machen, so dass ich es mir leisten kann.

I do not play an instrument but I love music. Firstly, I like electronic music because it's animated and energetic. When I go to the gym I listen to it so that I can run faster. Also music helps me to relax, for example after a stressful day at school what I like the most is to listen to favourite artist, Ed Sheeran. I want to see him live but first I have to do my chores so that I can afford it.

Pocket money and shopping

Ich habe Glück, weil meine Eltern mir dreißig Pfund pro Monat geben. Normalerweise kaufe ich Zeitschriften oder Videospiele, aber am vergangenen Wochenende verbrachte ich es beim Kinogehen mit meinen Freunden. Wenn ich die Chance hätte, hätte ich mehr Geld, so dass ich mehr Süßigkeiten kaufen könnte, aber meine Eltern meinen, dass ich genug Geld erhalte. Wie schrecklich! Ich glaube nicht, dass sie recht haben.

I am lucky because my parents give me thirty pounds a month. Normally, I buy magazines or videogames, but last weekend I spent it on going to the cinema with my friends. If I had the chance, I would like more money so that I can buy more sweets but I my parents think that I receive enough money. What a nightmare! I don't think they are right.

GLOSSARY OF IMPRESSIVE PHRASES

To be used to spice up your writing AS WELL AS your oral!

Use all your tenses

Present (including irregulars and reflexives) to describe what you normally do

Ich gehe ins Kino   *I go to the cinema*

ich mache meine Hausarbeiten   *I do my homework*

wir treffen uns am Wochenende   *We meet up at the weekend*

Ich ziehe mich an   *I get dressed*

AND with seit – ich wohne seit fünf Jahren hier

I have lived here for 5 years

Present continuous – there is no equivalent in German, so you have to accentuate the continuous element

Ich bin am Lesen/ich lese gerade   *I am reading*

Perfect to describe what you have done

Ich habe eine Menge Filme gesehen *I've seen a lot of films*

Ich habe Fotos gemacht   *I took photos*

ich habe gesonnt   *I sunbathed*

AND irregulars

Ich bin ins Kino gegangen   *I went to the cinema*

ich habe den Film nicht gemocht   *I didn't like the film*

ich habe meinen Eltern geholfen   *I helped my parents*

Pluperfect to describe what had happened before the action

Als wir zurückgekommen sind, hatte der Hund den Kuchen gefressen   *When we returned, the dog had eaten the cake*

Imperfect to describe repeated actions in the past or what life used to be like when you were younger

Ich wohnte auf dem Land   *I lived in the country*

ich sah jeden Tag fern   *I watched TV every day*

Als ich jünger war, ging Ich jeden dienstag tanzen

When I was younger, I used to go dancing every Tuesday

Ich durfte von Zeit zu Zeit Bonbons essen

I used to be allowed to eat sweets from time to time

Damals wusste ich nicht wie ungesund das war

Back then, I didn't know how unhealthy that was

Future tense to describe plans

Ich werde auf Urlaub gehen   *I am going to go on holiday*

Conditional to describe what would happen if certain conditions were fulfilled, and after "wenn" in sentences that begin with "if" in English

Ich möchte auf dem Land wohnen

I would like to live in the country

Ich würde in einem riesiggroßen Haus wohnen

I would live in an enormous house

Wenn ich könnte, würde ich die Uniform ändern

If I could I would change the uniform

Wenn ich reich wäre, würde ich ein Haus in Spanien kaufen

If I was rich I would buy a house in Spain

Es wäre schade, wenn wir an dem Planet, bleibende Schaden anrichten würden

It would be shame, if we did irreversible harm to the planet

Pluperfect after past conditional

Wenn ich es hätte machen können, hätte ich viel mehr unternommen

If I had been able to, I would have done much more

Present subjunctive with specific phrases

Seien wir vorsichtig!	*Let's be careful*
wie dem auch sei	*however that may be*
Ich denke, er habe recht	*I think he is right*

AND in indirect speech

Sie hat mir gesagt, sie sei müde	*She told me she was tired*

Using prepositions

Sich auf etwas freuen	*to look forward to*
Ich freue mich darauf	*I am looking forward to it*
Vor etwas Angst haben	*to be afraid of something*
Ich habe Angst vor der Zukunft	*I am afraid of the future*
Sich für etwas interessieren	*to be interested in*

Ich interessiere mich für	*I'm interested in*
Nach Hause gehen	*to go home*
Zu Hause bleiben	*to stay at home*
Medizin gegen etwas nehmen	*to take medicine for something*
gegen seine Zuckerkrankenheit	*for his diabetes*
An seiner Stelle	*in his shoes, in his place*
Ich habe auf den Film gewartet	*I waited for the film to come out*
Sie geht in die Küche	*she goes into the kitchen*
Wir essen in der Küche	*we eat in the kitchen*

Other verb structures

Ich werde gerade essen	*I am about to eat*
Ich habe eben gegessen	*I have just eaten*
Ich esse gerade	*I'm in the middle of eating*

Opinions

Meiner Meinung nach, …/ich bin der Meinung, dass…/ich glaube, dass….	*in my opinion*

Einerseits....andererseits	*On one hand ....on the other hand*
Im allgemein	*overall*

Positive opinions

Es lohnt sich	*it's worth it*
Das ist toll!	*That's great!*
Es freut mich	*it makes me happy*
Es bringt mich zum Lachen	*it makes me laugh*
Ich habe Lust, auf Urlaub zu gehen	*I feel like going on holiday*
Ich freue mich auf	*I'm looking forward to*
Ich habe Glück	*I am lucky*
Ich kriege gute Noten	*I get good marks*
Ich schaffe es ohne es/sie/ihn nicht	*I can't manage without it*
Wie wunderbar!	*How brilliant*
Das beste Land auf der Welt	*the best country in the world*
Ja, das stimmt	*Yes, that's true*
Doch!	*Yes it is! (emphatic)*
Es hat viel Spaß gemacht	*It was really fun*

ich habe mich sehr gefreut   *I really enjoyed it*

Was ich am meisten mag, ist/what mich am meisten freut, ist

what I like most is

Negative opinions

Was ich nicht mag, ist   *what I don't like is that*

Was mich beunruhigt ist   *what worries me most is that*

Es langt mir/ich habe genug davon   *I'm sick of it*

Ich kann es nicht ertragen   *I can't stand it*

Wie schrecklich!   *What a nightmare*

Wie furchtbar!   *How horrible!*

Expressions with haben

Ich habe Glück   *I'm lucky*

Ich hätte gern   *I would like*

Ich habe Hunger / Durst   *I'm hungry / thirsty*

Ich habe recht   *I'm right*

Ich habe Angst   *I am afraid*

Ich bin in Eile   *I'm in a hurry*

Gern

Ich höre gern Musik   *I love music*

Ich gehe nicht so gern in die Schule *I'm not that keen on school*

Comparatives and superlatives

Größer als   *bigger than him*

Weniger lustig als sie   *less fun than her*

Das Beste auf der Welt   *the best in the world*

Er ist genauso sportlich wie ich - he is as sporty as me

Seit / vor

Ich wohne seit 5 Jahren hier   *I have been living here 5 years*

Vor zwei Jahren bin ich nach Deutschland gegangen

Two years ago I went to Germany

Subjunctive expressions

Wenn ich viel Gelt hätte	*If I had a lot of money*
Wenn ich reich wäre	*If I was rich*
Wenn es mehr Fahrradwege gäbe	*If there were more cycle paths*
Wenn ich die Zeit gehabt hätte	*If I had had the time*
Wenn ich nur könnte!	*If only I could*

Um… zu + infinitive

Ich bin in den Park gegangen, um Tennis zu spielen

I went to the park to play tennis

Ohne…zu + infinitive

Die Jugendlichen nehmen Drogen, ohne sich auf die Konzequenzen zu überlegen

Young people take drugs without thinking about the consequences

Je ….. desto

Je mehr ich daran denke, desto pessimistisch werde ich

the more I think about it, the more pessimistic I become

Impersonal expressions

Man kann   *you can (one can)*

Man muss   *you must (one must)*

Linking words

jedoch   *however*

immerhin   *nevertheless*

Gerund as adjectives or adverbs

In German adverbs and adjectives are not as distinct as in English

dringend   *urgent/urgently*

entscheidend   *decisive/decisively*

spannend   *exciting/excitedly*

auffallend   *conspicuous/conspicuously*

MODALS IN ALL TENSES

Ich kann nicht schlafen   *I can't sleep*

Wir sollten Wasser sparen   *We should save water*

Ich könnte mehr Bewegung verschaffen   *I could do more exercise*

Ich darf viel fernsehen   *I'm allowed to watch a lot of TV*

Ich möchte Deutsch lernen   *I would like to learn German*

Ich will auf die Uni gehen   *I want to go to University*

GERMAN IDIOMS

Den Kürzeren ziehen   *to pull the short straw*

Hummeln im Hintern haben   *to have ants in your pants*

Mit jemandem durch dick und dünn gehen

to go through thick and thin with someone

Ein Sturm im Wasserglas   *storm in a teacup*

Eine Leiche im Keller haben   *to have a skeleton in your cupboard*

Einen Vogel haben   *to be a bit crazy*

Die Nase voll haben   *to be fed up*

Hals- und Beinbruch   *good luck!*

Wie ein Gott in Frankreich leben   *to live the life of Riley*

Ein Gedächtnis wie ein Elefant haben

to have the memory of an elephant

Die Spitze des Eisbergs	*the tip of the iceberg*
Auf Holz klopfen	*touch wood*
Einen grünen Daumen haben	*to be green-fingered*
Kalte Füße bekommen	*to get cold feet*
Wir ein Murmeltier schlafen	*to sleep like a log*

Thank you for purchasing this book. If you have any questions or comments, please do get in touch via my website www.lucymartintuition.co.uk

If you have found the book useful, please do leave us a review on Amazon, and if you are studying other languages, take a look at my other books in the series:

How to Ace your French oral

How to Ace your Spanish oral

French Vocabulary for GCSE

Spanish Vocabulary for GCSE

Common Entrance French Handbook

Printed in Great Britain
by Amazon